Mariana Becomes a Butterfly

An Agricultural Engineering Story

Written by the Engineering is Elementary Team

Illustrated by Jeannette Martin

Chapter One | Welcome to my Garden

I held my breath as I watched a speckled swallowtail butterfly crawling around the sunny yellow maguey flower in my garden.

In Spanish, the word for butterfly is *mariposa*. My name, Mariana, reminds me of that word. That's one of the reasons I like my name so much. Papá says that when I run around my garden I remind him of a butterfly, *una mariposa*, fluttering around.

Here in the Dominican Republic, people in the countryside enjoy beautiful

gardens year-round. Even in the capital city of Santo Domingo, people grow plants in pots. We have lots of warm, sunny weather, and most plants grow very well here.

But one plant in my garden is not doing well. It's my newest plant and one of my favorites—an ohelo berry plant. My friend Pablo got special permission to bring it back from Hawaii, where he went for vacation. At first, my ohelo plant grew tasty orange and red berries. But now the berries have all fallen off, and even though my plant still grows flowers, I can't get it to grow any new berries.

"Papá, my ohelo plant isn't growing berries. Do you think it's homesick?"

My father was weeding the vegetable garden. He walked over and gently lifted up a branch for inspection.

"That's a very good question, Mariana," he said. "Why don't we ask Tía Letitia the next time we see her?"

"Great idea!" I said. "Tía Leti will know just what to do."

My aunt Letitia, or Tía Leti in Spanish, is an agricultural engineer. An engineer, Tía Leti says, uses her creativity and her knowledge of science, math, and materials to solve problems. Agricultural engineers work with biology and the natural world. Tía Leti does a lot of work with plants, especially plants that we use for food. I'm sure she'll be able to help me with my ohelo plant.

Chapter Two | My Plant Puzzle

"Tía Leti!" I called from her front walkway. She came outside and gave me a big hug.

"How are you, Mariana?" Tía Leti asked.

"I have a puzzle for you," I said. "Papá said you could help me with it."

We sat down at the table in Tía Leti's backyard. The plants in her garden were in full bloom. Everywhere I looked there were splashes and dots of blue, yellow, orange, red, and green. As the flowers swayed back and forth in the breeze, they looked like fluttering butterfly wings.

"So what is this puzzle, Mariana?" asked Tía Leti.

I explained the problems I was having with my ohelo plant.

"I have been watering it and taking extra special care of it, but it's no use."

"That is a puzzle!" Tía Leti said. "But it's one I bet we can solve, if we ask some good questions. Do you know how plants make seeds?"

I nodded eagerly. "Yes, Papá told me. It starts with pollination."

"That's right," Tía Leti said. She had on her teacher face now. Tía Leti loves to teach me new things. "But do you know how pollination works?"

I nodded. "Sometimes, when an insect lands on a plant, the pollen sticks to the insect. I've seen it happen with bees and butterflies on my maguey flowers. If the pollen stuck to the insect falls off onto another maguey flower, that maguey can make seeds. Remember, Papá, that time I got pollen all over my nose?"

Once, I had put my nose into a flower to smell how sweet it was. When I pulled away from the flower, Papá laughed and pointed at my face. I had yellow powder, like fine flour, on my nose. I had picked up pollen from the flower!

"What a good memory you have, Mariana. You were just a little *mariposa* then," Papá said.

"In many plants that have berries," Tía Leti explained, "the seeds are inside the berries."

"So that's why there were little seeds in my ohelo berries," I said. "If my plant is having trouble making new seeds, does that mean it isn't being pollinated?"

"That's an interesting guess—a hypothesis," said Tía Leti. "Scientists and engineers like me make hypotheses when we have ideas we want to test. Can you think of a way to test your hypothesis?"

"I could watch my ohelo plant to see if any insects visit it and pollinate it," I said.

Tía Leti reached into her bag and pulled out a notebook. "An engineer like you will certainly need a place to take notes about what you see. You can have this journal to record your observations."

"Thank you, Tía Leti," I said. "I can't wait to get started!"

Chapter Three | Watching the Insects

Each day as I took care of my garden, I observed which plants the insects visited. I drew pictures of the insects, kept track of how many I saw, and wrote down what they did.

By watching the insects in my garden very carefully, I made some new discoveries. I've always spent so much time watching butterflies flutter around that I didn't realize butterflies in all different stages of life lived in my garden. Butterflies start their lives inside tiny little eggs. I found some hiding underneath the leaves of one of my plants. They don't look much like the eggs we eat for breakfast. They look soft, like jelly.

Out of an egg comes a larva. We call it a caterpillar. I watched a little caterpillar crawl across a shiny green plant

leaf. The caterpillar munches on leaves to grow fat and healthy. When it is ready, the caterpillar becomes a pupa. The pupa develops inside a shiny little sac called a chrysalis. Finally it emerges as a colorful butterfly. As I watched the caterpillar inch across the leaf, chomping away, I wondered what color wings it would grow.

I wonder if the insects in my garden ever watch me grow? As I get bigger each year, my legs and arms get longer, and sometimes I change the way I wear my hair. But I still look like Mariana. As butterflies go through metamorphosis—the changes in their bodies as they grow—they look very different in each stage of their lives.

A passion flower butterfly fluttered over and landed on the same bush where I was watching the caterpillar. I slowly crouched down next to the plant so I wouldn't scare the butterfly. Its body was glossy black, with tiny, fuzzy hairs covering its thin legs. The butterfly's beautiful wings were still. It's hard to imagine that those paper-thin wings let the butterfly move through the air almost like magic.

I looked back at the roly-poly caterpillar moving across the leaf. Was the caterpillar looking at the butterfly just like I was? I wondered if the caterpillar knew that someday it would have wings and fly, too.

The week passed. I saw insects visit my maguey flowers, my orchids, and my white plumeria flowers. Bees visited. Butterflies visited. Even some flies visited. But not one insect visited my ohelo plant.

Chapter Four | A Natural System

When Tía Leti came to our house, I brought her out to the garden. I showed her the pictures in my garden journal.

"I'm impressed," Tía Leti said. "You are a careful observer. I can tell by the details you put in your journal. Did you find any clues that might help solve your plant puzzle?"

"I didn't see any insects visit my new plant."

"Hmm," Tía Leti said. "Why do you suppose that's so?"

"I'm not sure," I said. "But it made me wonder what attracts the bees and butterflies to my other plants. I know the plants need insects to pollinate them. But why do the insects need plants?"

Tía Leti put on her teacher face. "Let's use what you know to make some thoughtful guesses. I'll help you. Inside some flowers is a sweet liquid called nectar." She picked a flower from one of my plants. Carefully, she pulled the petals away and let a few drops of liquid trickle out of the flower. "Some insects eat nectar as food," Tía Leti explained. "Can you see it inside this flower?"

I squinted. There it was—way down deep inside the petals.

"It's wrapped up like a little present in the flower," I said. "So when insects visit my flowers, they're coming to eat?"

Tía Leti nodded. "Pollination is an amazing natural system. All the parts work together. The insects visit the flowers so they can drink the nectar inside. By chance, they pick up pollen while they're eating at one flower, and bring it to the next flower when they stop to eat again. Pollination is important for the plants, and getting food is important for the insect."

"So the plants get pollinated, and then they can make seeds that make more plants and more pollen," I said. "And the insects get fed, so they can be healthy and do more pollinating!"

"Exactly," Tía Leti said.

I picked a small, delicate ohelo blossom and carefully pulled the petals away. A bit of sweet nectar trickled out.

"There's nectar in the ohelo flowers. Why won't the insects come eat it?"

"Well, imagine that you came over to my house for dinner," Tía Leti said, "and on the table I laid out some food. But I put all the food in the very center of the table where you couldn't reach it. Do you think you would have a very good dinner?"

"If I couldn't get to the food, I'd still be hungry!"

"And do you think you would come back for dinner again?" she asked.

"No, I'd go to dinner at someone else's house." I said.

"Exactly," Tía Leti said. "I think the same thing is happening to the insects with your new plant. That plant

is from another place. Insects here on our island might not have the right mouth parts to reach into the ohelo flower to get the nectar. For them, it's like your new plant's nectar is out of reach in the center of the table! They'll visit other plants to get food. And if they don't visit your new plant, they don't help pollinate it and it can't grow new berries."

Thoughts were fluttering through my head. "If there is an insect in Hawaii that pollinates my plant, maybe I could bring that insect here to help me."

"That's an interesting thought," said Tía Leti. "I'm working on a project in my lab right now that might help you think a bit more about that idea. Tomorrow you can visit me at work to learn more about it."

Chapter Five | Finding Balance

The next day I put on my nicest outfit to visit Tía Leti at the university. I got to see her office and meet some of the people she works with before she took me outside to a papaya orchard.

"This is where we test many of our ideas." Tía Leti inspected one of the beautiful orange papayas above her head. She reached up and plucked it from a low branch.

My mouth watered. Sweet papaya is my favorite breakfast. But when Tía Leti turned the papaya over, I saw that it had a wormhole in it. "Oh, no," I cried, "there's a mealybug in the papaya!" I had seen mealybugs eating the fruit on the papaya tree in our backyard. Once they get inside, the fruit is not good for people anymore.

"When I was a little girl, there were no mealybugs in the Dominican Republic," Tía Leti said. "The papaya mealybug's original home is in Mexico. But a few years ago, the papaya mealybug showed up here. It started feasting on our papaya fruits. The mealybugs were getting happy and fat, but the insects ruined the papayas for people."

"Poor papayas," I said. "And poor people! What could we do?"

"One thing we could do is spray chemicals that kill insects, called pesticides, on the trees," said Tía Leti. "But some pesticides that we use can also be harmful to people."

"And what if some other insects, like butterflies, landed on the papaya tree? Could the pesticides hurt them, too? I asked.

"Good question, my little butterfly," said Tía Leti. "They could hurt them. We did some research and found that instead of using chemicals to kill the mealybugs, we could get help from another insect. There's a certain type of wasp that kills the mealybug. If we release enough of those wasps they would stop the mealybugs from destroying so many papayas. We call this Integrated Pest Management. It's another natural system—a system that uses the processes of nature instead of processes created by people."

"A natural system—just like pollination," I said. "So that wasp helped balance the environment again."

"Very good, Mariana," said Tía Leti. "The environment has many natural systems that maintain their own special balance."

Tía Leti's explanation made sense. But something still bothered me. "Wait a minute, Tía Leti," I said. "If I could bring an insect here from Hawaii to pollinate my plant, the insect might be helpful, like the wasp. But what if it's

like the mealybug and causes lots of problems? It could upset the balance of the environment. I still don't know how to help my plant."

"Keep thinking, Mariana," Tía Leti said. "If one solution does not work, then you need to think of a different one. Let's take a walk into my lab. I want to show you something that I think might help you engineer a solution to your pollination problem."

Chapter Six | Becoming a Butterfly

Inside Tía Leti's laboratory, plants were all over the windowsills and tables. We sat down in front of a frangipani plant with little yellow flowers. They looked like tiny stars peeking through the plant's green leaves.

I thought for a minute. "My ohelo plant is missing part of its pollination system. The insects here are not helping to pollinate my plant. If I can't bring an insect here to fix the system, is there some way I can fix it myself? Can I pretend to be a butterfly and pollinate my ohelo?"

"Now you are thinking like an engineer," said Tía Leti. "In my laboratory we have some plants like your ohelo plant." She led me to a funny cone-shaped plant with deep red flowers. "This plant does not have a natural pollinator here in the Dominican Republic. We agricultural engineers need to act like insects to pollinate it."

"You pretend to be butterflies here in your lab?" I asked. I pictured Tía Leti and her coworkers fluttering around the lab with giant wings.

"In a way we do," said Tía Letitia. "We use a little tool with a fuzzy surface or texture to act like butterfly legs and carry pollen."

"I could do that," I said excitedly. "Then I would be the pollinating *mariposa* for my ohelo plant!"

Tía Leti picked up a small stick from the table next to her and handed it to me. There was a fuzzy ball on the end of the stick. "This is the technology we use here to pollinate plants," she said.

"This is technology?" I asked. "It doesn't look like technology."

Tía Leti smiled. "Technology is anything that humans make to help solve problems."

"I don't think this tool would help me, though," I said. "The flowers on my ohelo plant are small. I would need a smaller pollinator."

Tía Leti nodded. "I think you're right. But you can design your own hand pollinator. You've already shown me that you have all the skills you need to be a good engineer."

My mind was buzzing like a beehive. "I know what size pollinator I will need, but I'll have to look carefully at the shape of the ohelo flowers, too. And I'll need to find a material that has the right texture to pick up the pollen and drop it off on another flower."

"That's very smart, Mariana. You can use your imagination and think of lots of ideas. Then you can create and test your design to make sure it will work. It might take a few tries. If your first design doesn't work, you can always improve it or try another one. Engineers use all of the steps in the engineering design process when we are solving problems." Tía Leti smiled at me. "I'm really proud of you, Mariana!"

I couldn't wait to begin designing my own pollinator.

Chapter Seven | A Design that Works

All day long I worked on the design of my hand pollinator. I tested different materials to see which had the best texture for picking up and dropping off pollen. After I figured out which material worked the best, I made a handle for my pollinator that would let me reach into the ohelo flowers.

Now, here it is, six weeks later. And guess what? My plant has started to grow berries again. My pollinator worked! I can't wait to pick some berries to give to Tía Leti.

Now I'm exploring pollinators for other plants. I can make changes to my design that make the pollinators work better for different types of plants. Each plant has its own pollinator.

Sometimes I think about that day in the lab, when Tía Leti told me we were going to pretend to be insects. At first I thought she meant we would flutter around, flapping our colorful wings. But for my ohelo plant, I really am its pollinating *mariposa*!

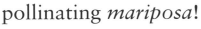

Try It!
Design a Hand Pollinator

You can design a hand pollinator, just like Mariana. There are many ways for plants to be pollinated: wind, birds, and insects are just a few. Have you ever seen insects visit a flower? What makes insects good pollinators? Your goal is to design a hand pollinator for a specific flower shape.

Materials
- ☐ Baking soda
- ☐ Construction paper
- ☐ Cellophane tape
- ☐ Aluminum foil
- ☐ Pipe cleaner
- ☐ Pom poms
- ☐ Craft stick
- ☐ String
- ☐ Test tube

Find a Flower
Think about what your pollinator needs to do. What is the shape of the flower you are designing? Select a flower from your yard or a flower shop. Or, you can make a model of a flower. Try one of these options:

A. Cut out a flower shape from dark construction paper and cover the center with a thin coat of baking soda to represent a flat flower, such as a poppy.

B. Fill the bottom of a test tube with baking soda to represent a tube-shaped flower such as a Dutchman's Pipe.

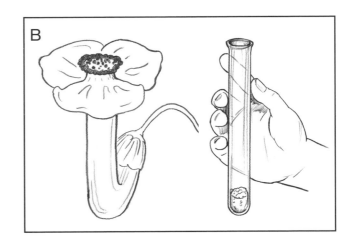

Test the Materials

Do you think aluminum foil would do a good job of picking up and dropping off pollen? How about a pipe cleaner? Using a small amount of each material, pretend that it is an insect visiting a flower coated with pollen. Spread a little baking soda on a flat surface and pretend that it is pollen. Now try to pick up the baking soda with each of the materials. How much baking soda (pollen) does each material pick up? Try tapping the material gently against your finger. How much of the baking soda (pollen) falls off? Which material will you use to design your hand pollinator?

Design a Hand Pollinator

Look again at your flower. Where is the pollen located in the flower blossom? Design a hand pollinator for your flower that will pick up and drop off pollen. Test your design.

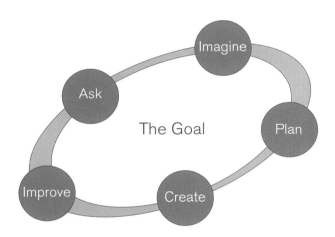

Improve your Pollinator

Use the engineering design process to improve your hand pollinator. Can you use your hand pollinator for more than one type of flower?

See What Others Have Done

See what other kids have done at http://www.mos.org/eie/tryit. What did you try? You can submit your solutions and pictures to our website, and maybe we'll post your submission!

Glossary

Agricultural Engineer: An engineer who designs solutions to problems concerning living systems or biology.

Engineer: A person who uses his or her knowledge of math, science, materials, and creativity to solve problems.

Engineering Design Process: The steps that engineers use to design something to solve a problem.

Frangipani: A plant with small yellow or cream-colored star-shaped flowers that is native to warm, tropical areas, such as the Caribbean. Pronounced *FRAN-jeh-PAN-ee*.

Hand Pollinator: A tool used by people to accomplish pollination in the absence of a natural pollinator.

Hypothesis: A proposed explanation for a fact or observation.

Insect: A small animal with three body sections, three pairs of legs, and a skeleton on the outside of its body.

Integrated Pest Management: An insect control system that relies on natural systems.

Mariposa: Spanish word for butterfly. Pronounced *MAR-ee-poe-sa*.

Maguey: A yellow puffball-shaped flower found in the Dominican Republic. Pronounced *MAG-wee*.

Metamorphosis: The transition of an insect from egg to larva to pupa to adult.

Nectar: A sweet liquid inside some flowers and plants that attracts pollinators.

Ohelo: A berry plant found in Hawaii. Pronounced *o-HAY-low*.

Pesticide: A chemical that is used to control insect populations.

Pollination: The transfer of pollen from the male part of a flower to the female part, that results in the growth of new seeds.

Technology: Any thing, process, or system that people create and use to solve a problem.

Texture: The appearance and feel of a surface.